ChrisGoodeandCompany

THE ADVENTURES OF WOUND MAN AND SHIRLEY

by Chris Goode

The original production of *The Adventures of Wound Man and Shirley* was first performed at Contact, Manchester on 23 April 2009

Writer / Director / Performer / Sound Design – **Chris Goode**
Designer – **Janet Bird**
Lighting Designer – **Anna Watson**
Animator – **Adam Smith**
Associate Artist – **Jonny Liron**
Stage Manager / Set Builder – **James Lewis**
Technical Manager – **Andy Purves**
Relighting Technician – **Anthony Newton**
Associate Designer – **Andrew Riley**
Multimedia Consultant – **Liam Jarvis**
Producer – **Ric Watts**

This revised version of *The Adventures of Wound Man and Shirley* was first performed at Pleasance Courtyard, Edinburgh on 20 August 2011

Writer / Performer / Sound Design – **Chris Goode**
Director – **Wendy Hubbard**
Designer and Lighting Designer – **James Lewis**
Producer – **Ric Watts**

Commissioned by Queer Up North International Festival

The original 2009 production was a Ric Watts and Queer Up North co-production in association with Contact, funded by Arts Council England.

The revised 2011 version is a Chris Goode & Company production.

Thanks to: The original creative and production team for the show, Jonathan Best and all at Queer Up North, everyone at Contact, Frantic Assembly, Royal Exchange Theatre, Simon Curtis, Beccy Smith, Stuart Heyes, Analogue, Sue Lewis, Roddy Gauld and Arts Council England, Rebecca Glover, Austin Lewis, Anna Goodman, Greg McLaren and everyone at Stoke Newington International Airport, Pleasance, Giles Smart, Mobius Industries and all at Oberon Books.

CHRIS GOODE & COMPANY

Chris Goode & Company is a new company formed by lead artist Chris Goode and producer Ric Watts to develop original collaborative and exploratory theatre projects across a variety of forms and contexts.

In recent years, Chris has worked prolifically across the UK with his shows being produced by some of the country's leading theatres – such as the Drum Theatre, Plymouth; Royal & Derngate, Northampton; Ustinov Studio, Bath and The Gate, London.

Chris Goode & Company has been established to provide a home for a broad range of (often uncategorisable) performance projects, principally focused on ensemble-based collaborative and participatory processes, and on formally innovative but accessible approaches to documentary and storytelling.

The company launched in March 2011 and projects to date include:

A new version of Chris's acclaimed solo storytelling show, *The Adventures of Wound Man and Shirley*. Developed at Stoke Newington International Airport and premiered at Pleasance, Edinburgh, August 2011.

Keep Breathing, a new solo interactive documentary performance about the science and ecology of breathing. A Drum Theatre Plymouth production, created with the support of London Word Festival. Premieres November 2011, touring from 2012.

Open House, a participatory ensemble residency project for the Transform season at West Yorkshire Playhouse, June 2011.

A number of other projects are already in development for 2012 and beyond.

Whether in solo or group formats, the company's work is always collaboratively created by a fluid, constantly evolving ensemble of performers and makers, with Chris Goode's role as lead artist setting a characteristic tone of openness, friendliness and restless invention.

To find out more about **Chris Goode & Company**, and its work, past present and future, please visit:

www.chrisgoodeandcompany.co.uk

BIOGRAPHIES

Chris Goode

Chris Goode is a writer, director, performer and sound designer, who has been described as 'one of the most exciting talents working in Britain today' (*Guardian*) and 'an extremely highly regarded alternative theatre maker' (Caroline McGinn, *Time Out*).

His work has included two Fringe First award-winning shows: *Neutrino* (with Unlimited Theatre: Soho Theatre, London, and international tour), and his own solo debut *Kiss Of Life* (Pleasance, Edinburgh; Drill Hall, London), which in 2007 travelled to Sydney Opera House as part of the Sydney International Festival.

In 2008 he won the inaugural Headlong / Gate New Directions Award for his production …*Sisters* at the Gate Theatre. More recently he was part of the international touring cast of Tim Crouch's controversial and acclaimed play *The Author*, winner of the John Whiting Award and a Total Theatre Award for Innovation.

Other notable recent work has included: *Open House* (West Yorkshire Playhouse); *Keep Breathing* (London Word Festival); *Who You Are* (Tate Modern) and *Where You Stand* (Contact, Manchester); *Glass House* (Royal Opera House Covent Garden); *Landscape / Monologue* (Ustinov, Bath); *The Adventures of Wound Man and Shirley* (UK tour for Queer Up North); *Hey Mathew* (Theatre in the Mill, Bradford); *King Pelican* and *Speed Death Of The Radiant Child* (Drum Theatre, Plymouth); *Longwave* (Lyric, Hammersmith); *Homemade* (Cork Midsummer Festival); *Escapology* (Newbury Comedy Festival).

Chris is currently an Artsadmin Associate Artist. He has previously been Associate Researcher at Rose Bruford College, and is highly in demand as a lecturer and workshop leader. Chris's *The History of Airports: Selected texts for performance 1995-2009* was published in 2009 by Ganzfeld. As a poet he has published three chapbooks with Barque Press, and he has recently edited *Better Than Language: An anthology of new modernist poetries* for Ganzfeld.

He blogs at the widely read Thompson's Bank of Communicable Desire (http://beescope.blogspot.com)

Ric Watts

Ric Watts is a producer based in Manchester. He is currently Producer/Company Director of Analogue, having developed and toured all of the company's critically acclaimed work to date: *Mile End, Beachy Head, Lecture Notes on a Death Scene, Living Film Set* and *2401 Objects*. As a founding member of Chris Goode & Company, he has produced *The Adventures of Wound Man and Shirley (*UK Tour, Edinburgh*), The End of the World Filmed by the Angel of Notre Dame,* and *Open House.*

Ric recently became Producer for Unlimited Theatre, with who he produced *Mission To Mars* (Polka/UK Tour) and with who he is currently developing a portfolio of mid-scale projects. Ric is also Producer for The Frequency D'ici, having produced the award-winning *Paperweight* and *Free Time Radical.*

He started his career as Producer at Your Imagination, where he developed new work by Cartoon de Salvo (*The Sunflower Plot, The Chaingang Gang*), Ridiculusmus (*The Importance of Being Earnest*), Kazuko Hohki (*Evidence for the Existence of Borrowers*), and Your Imagination / BAC (*The Ratcatcher of Hamelin*).

Since 2006, Ric has been working as an independent producer and notable independent productions include: *FOOD* by theimaginarybody (Traverse, UK tour); *Particularly in the Heartland* by The TEAM (UK Tour), *FIT* by Rikki Beadle-Blair / Queer Up North, *Flathampton* for Royal & Derngate, *The Knowledge Emporium* by Slung Low, *Running on Air* by Laura Mugridge (Edinburgh, UK Tour) and *Avon Calling* by The Other Way Works.

During 2008-09, Ric was Producer for Schtanhaus, the producing partnership between Tom Morris and Emma Stenning. For Schtanhaus, he primarily produced the work of Filter Theatre, including *Twelfth Night* (Tricycle/UK and international tour).

Ric was Festival Producer for the 2010 Queer Up North International Festival – following four years of previous involvement as Associate Producer. During his year artistically leading the organisation he commissioned five new pieces, including work by Quarantine, Starving Artists and Bourgeois and Maurice, and brought international artists such as Ontroerend Goed, Peggy Shaw , Taylor Mac and Justin Bond to Manchester.

Wendy Hubbard

Wendy Hubbard is a theatre maker, specialising in devised performance. Since 2002 she has been co-Artistic Director of the theatre company Mapping4D, winners of the 2004 Oxford Samuel Beckett Theatre Trust Award with *The Pink Bits*, which was performed at Riverside Studios.

She has worked as director, assistant director and dramaturg with Chris Goode on several productions, including *The Adventures of Wound Man and Shirley* (Pleasance, Edinburgh), ...*Sisters* (Gate / Headlong) and *Kiss Of Life* (Sydney Opera House), and a number of research and development projects (including NT Studio, Royal Court and Headlong).

She is currently working as a collaborator / dramaturg with Melanie Wilson on *Autobiographer*, and other recent work includes projects with Finlay Robertson, Heather Uprichard, Lucy Ellinson and Jamie Wood.

She is currently a PhD student at Queen Mary, University of London.

James Lewis

James Lewis is a set designer and builder working mainly in theatre.

For Chris Goode & Company he has worked on *The Adventures of Wound Man and Shirley* (Pleasance, Edinburgh) and *Keep Breathing* (London Word Festival), and as one of the five collaborators in the core team for *Open House* (West Yorkshire Playhouse). Previous work with Chris includes *Kiss Of Life* (Sydney Opera House) and *Longwave* (Lyric Hammersmith).

Other current and recent projects include work with The Frequency D'ici, Niki McCretton, Guy Dartnell, Toby Wilsher, and Plested and Brown.

A NOTE ON THE MUSIC IN THE SHOW

Right from the start in making this piece, music was always crucial to the way we created a distinct and detailed world for Shirley to live in.

This is a list of the music used in the current version of the show. Makers of any subsequent production are free to use whatever music they like, but this may be a useful reference or starting-point.

Baxendale, 'Keep Feeling (Fascination)'
from *Reproductions: Songs of the Human League* (What Are Records)

Tricky, 'Ponderosa [Original Instrumental]'
from *Ponderosa [single]* (Island)

Adem, 'To Cure A Weakling Child + Boy/Girl Song'
from *Takes* (Domino)

Flaming Lips, 'Vein of Stars'
from *At War With the Mystics* (Warner Bros.)

Jazz Mandolin Project, 'Everything In Its Right Place'
from *The Deep Forbidden Lake* (Lenapee)

Nena, 'Friday I'm In Love'
from *Cover Me* (Warner)

Rice and Beans Orchestra, 'Catano Ferry'
from *Rice and Beans Orchestra* (T.K. Records)

Pipas, 'Tout Va Bien'
from *Chunnel Autumnal* (Matinee Recordings)

Jim O'Rourke, 'Prelude to 110 or 220 / Women of the World'
from *Eureka* (Domino)

mr_hopkinson's computer, 'Roads'
http://www.computersings.com

Opsvik & Jennings, 'Commuter Anthem'
from *Commuter Anthems* (Rune Grammofon)

Brigada Victor Jara, 'Arriba Monte'
from *Por Sendas, Montes E Vales* (Farol Música)

Richard Butler, 'Milk'
from *Richard Butler* (Koch)

Bloc Party, 'Positive Tension (Go! Team Remix)'
from *Silent Alarm Remixed* (Wichita)

Human League, 'Human'
from *Crash* (Virgin)

Westlife feat. Mariah Carey, 'Against All Odds
(Take A Look At Me Now)'
from *Coast to Coast* (Sony/BMG)

Kate Rusby, 'Underneath the Stars'
from *Underneath the Stars* (Pure Records)

Brian Eno, 'How Many Worlds'
from *Another Day on Earth* (Hannibal)

Nena, 'Helden [Heroes]'
from *Cover Me* (Warner)

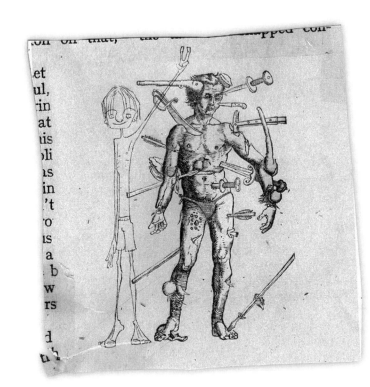

Chris Goode

THE ADVENTURES OF WOUND MAN AND SHIRLEY

OBERON BOOKS
LONDON
WWW.OBERONBOOKS.COM

First published in 2011 by Oberon Books Ltd
521 Caledonian Road, London N7 9RH
Tel: +44 (0) 20 7607 3637 / Fax: +44 (0) 20 7607 3629
e-mail: info@oberonbooks.com
www.oberonbooks.com

A catalogue record for this book is available from the British Library.

ISBN: 978-1-84943-180-4

Cover design by Liam Jarvis
Shirley drawn by Adam Smith

Printed and bound by CPI Group (UK) Ltd, Croydon, CR0 4YY.

Introduction.

Hello. Thanks for being here.

The story I want to tell you this evening is kind of a love story.

When I was writing it, I started by thinking about the first time I fell in love.

I was fourteen and he was fourteen and he had a girlfriend and I was sighing a lot. And at breaktime we'd sit on the window ledge together and share the headphones of his Walkman; he'd have one ear and I'd have the other. So together we both made stereo.

Every day I thought my heart would burst.

I still think about him. He's married now. He has kids and pets.

And there was someone else I met at around the same time. In history class.

I have a picture of him. So you can meet him too. You might have seen him before.

Everybody. Meet Wound Man.

This is an illustration from the early 16th century, it pops up in medical / surgical textbooks, accompanying information about how to treat all these different injuries that might befall a person in a battle.

I don't know if you can see, I think he looks a bit like Bill Murray. Crossed with a Swiss Army knife.

I still think about Wound Man too. I always remembered him. I always found him touching.

So when I started thinking about writing this, I thought, if anybody looks like they belong in a love story…

So this is a story about Wound Man.

(Music.)

And about a skinny fourteen-year-old boy called Shirley.

This is the music for the start of the story. We're not going to play it too loud. Because at the start of the story, Shirley's asleep in bed.

Settle back and I'll tell you the whole thing.

One.

Shirley opens his eyes and looks up at the stars.

This moment makes no sound.

The moment when this kid called Shirley opens his eyes, wakes up in his bed, in his bedroom, in the attic conversion of a three-up two-down house, on a twitchy-curtained cul-de-sac shaped like a hockey stick, right on the edge of a little town you've never even heard of, somewhere in England, on the outskirts of Europe, in the world, in the solar system, out in the suburbs of the Milky Way, the universe, for ever and ever, infinity and no returns.

Stars.

On his bedroom ceiling.

The pack said they'd glow in the dark, but they never really have. This is something that Shirley frets about whenever he goes out in the evening. What if the stars on his ceiling are glowing right now and there's no one there to see?

They've been up there for years, these stars, and he knows they're childish, but he likes to open his eyes and see them.

Immediately he starts to run through the constellations in his head, like a roll call.

The Big Dipper and the Little Dipper. The Giraffe and the Dragon. Cepheus and Cassiopeia. Andromeda and the Lizard.

He likes that the stars are there. He likes that that's the first thing he thinks about when he opens his eyes. Because then, the thing that he doesn't want to be the first thing he thinks about, is only the second thing. And the other thing he doesn't want to think about becomes the third thing, and by then it's time to get up and hit the shower.

You can think about the third thing in the shower, that's true.

Sometimes you can't not think about the third thing.

But for now, Shirley's lying in bed, naming the constellations to himself. And it's making no sound.

For some reason he's woken up a whole hour early.

Outside it's already light. It's a beautiful morning.

He feels like something's not quite right.

But that's not an unusual start to the day for Shirley.

For a moment he panics. He rolls over on to the edge of the bed and checks underneath.

It's there. It's OK. Stop panicking, Shirley. Why wouldn't it be OK?

It's not OK.

He sits on the edge of the bed, and pulls the case all the way out, and picks it up by the handle, and rests it on his knees. The feel of the case against his bare skin. The black moulded plastic, cold and hard and yet it feels so intimate. The warmth inside it. It's like hugging a naked statue and wishing it would come to life.

He runs his fingers over it. His fingers instinctively know how much more precious this object is than anyone else could possibly understand. Even the people at school who think Shirley's the biggest wuss of all time would be shocked if they knew how gentle he is when he touches this plastic case.

He's trying, like he always tries, to make it enough to just touch. You don't have to open it, Shirley. You don't have to look inside. You don't have to undo the clips.

Hit the shower, Shirley.

He undoes the clips. He opens the case just a tiny bit.

Once it's open it's open.

He can't not check. He opens the lid all the way and checks.

It takes two seconds.

He closes the lid.

That sinking feeling.

He does the clips up again. Slides the case back underneath his bed.

Then he sits with his elbows on his knees and his chin in his hands. He's so bony.

Why did you have to check? You idiot.

His brain wants to think about everything suddenly. The first thing the second thing the third thing. Everything.

And then it all stops and Shirley realizes why he's been feeling all this time like there's something not quite right.

He becomes aware of a sound in the road outside. It's been vaguely there since he woke up. Maybe it's the reason he woke up so early in the first place.

This funny sort of clankity-clunking sound, like pots and pans, like the half a kitchen that they tied to the back of his uncle's car on the day he got married, driving off down the lane all clankity-clunk in a clapped-out Herbie the Love Bug car with these saucepans trailing behind, and Shirley, who was seven years old at the time, the only one in the whole family who either knew or cared that the sign that they'd put on the back wasn't spelt right. Going off on honeymoon with a sign on the back that says JUST MARIED. Clankity-clunk.

That's the sound that's coming down the cul-de-sac shaped like a hockey stick, six in the morning.

Shirley gets up, pads over to his window, and surveys the road below.

The source of the sound is right there, passing underneath the window, so amazingly visible that Shirley can't see it. He looks over one way, back the other way. Maybe it's a dog that's playing with a hubcap, or a milkfloat with a puncture.

It takes ages for his brain to go, Shirley! Look!

What the heck – ?

It's a man, just a regular guy, maybe fortysomething, short, neat hair. Is he… actually… naked? No, not quite, he's wearing some kind of silver… thong. Like a bodybuilder's posing pouch.

But that's the least of it.

All over his body: weapons. Sticking out at crazy angles like the cocktail sticks in a cheese and pineapple hedgehog at a little kid's birthday.

His whole body a torture chamber. A dagger here, a scimitar there, a clawhammer digging deep in his shoulder, shrapnel and arrowheads, a spear in his thigh, a javelin penetrating his foot, a sword that passes right through his middle. Just under his left eye, what looks like a little kitchen knife for doing your sprouts. It's the backs of Shirley's legs that notice, before his brain has even registered, how the man's right hand is hanging off at the wrist. He can see the wires of gristle that are just about holding it on.

Shirley's mind is racing: should he run down and help, should he call the police, should he go back to bed and assume he's still dreaming? He listens to the clankity-clunk as the poor man makes his snail's-pace way down the street, with the weapons all boinking together as he moves, slap-bang in the middle of the birdless silence of dawn in the cul-de-sac. 6:05 in the morning and it's just Shirley in nothing but his boxers, skinny in the window, and the morning and the day ahead.

At last the man arrives at the front door of number 23, where no one has lived for a while. Shirley watches him unhook a key from the end of the handle of a stiletto knife that's sticking in his side. The man opens his front door, turns sideways to negotiate the threshold, and disappears inside.

At that moment, Shirley notices a movement, like a soundless twitch in the corner of the picture. He can't be sure, but he's sure enough for a story like this: it's a tremor behind the venetian blind of the man in the house next door at number 22, Reg Parsley. Everybody knows Reg Parsley, he's the *grand fromage* of the local neighbourhood watch, and he takes his duties very seriously. So it stands to reason he'll have been watching the new guy staggering home at daybreak making a clankity-clunk in a built-up area.

Shirley's curiosity likewise is pounding in his chest. This man with the weapons and the silver thong. He resolves to go round to number 23 later and just say hello, and the thought of it alone makes him happy for a moment.

And then he thinks.

Reg Parsley.

Was he watching the man coming home?

Or was he watching me watching?

Did he see me in the window?

Oh, what does it matter if he did, thinks Shirley, as he starts to get dressed, in a hurry all of a sudden.

Two.

(Doorbell.)

One, says Shirley in his head.

Two. He's decided he's going to count up to…

Three. …ten, and if there's no answer by…

Four. …ten, then he's just going to go a-

Five. -way again and forget all about the

Six. weird hallucination that he had this morning.

Seven.

Eight. Mind your own beeswax Mr Parsley.

Nine. Nine already. He's half-disappointed, half-relieved.

Ten.

So none of it really happened. Of course it didn't. How can it have? Well, good…

…Eleven.

Twelve, the door opens, on a chain like old ladies have. All Shirley can see is the hilt of a sword wobbling at eye-level.

– Yes? says a voice behind the door.

– Oh…, says Shirley. He should've gone on ten. – I'm sorry to disturb you…

– Yes, well you have rather, says the man. To be honest.

– Only I'm… I'm doing a sponsored…

Shirley's mind goes blank.

– What? Walk? Swim? What?

– …Silence, says Shirley.

And out of his back pocket he produces the fake sponsorship form that he's just spent an hour doing on the computer. He holds the form up to the chink in the door.

– Silence, says the man. Mm. Tricky business. You'd better come in.

He takes off the chain and opens the door. Shirley steps inside. The hallway is a bit of a squeeze, the man has to shuffle ahead. He's still all covered in weaponry. Still got the thong. Only difference is carpet slippers. Comfy ones like Shirley's mum's.

– It's a bit of a mess, I'm afraid, I'm still unpacking. Boxes, look. Come on through to the kitchen.

– When did you move in? says Shirley.

– Last week, says the man. Early days.

– Why did you want to live around here? says Shirley. – It's horrible.

– Well I'm sure it's going to suit me. It's very peaceful here, that's what I'm after. Fresh start, you know. Clean slate.

The kitchen feels crowded, just the two of them and the ironing board, with a row of identical silver thongs all lined up ready to be ironed. Shirley looks around the room for a moment. His eye comes to rest on a postcard stuck to the door of the fridge. It's a teenage actor he vaguely recognizes, from the old days. Like the 90s or something. Died of drugs.

– And if you're going to do this sponsored silence, says the man, that's all going to help on the peace and quiet front, isn't it? How long are you planning to do? A month? Two months?

Shirley giggles.

– My mum says if I last more than twenty minutes she's calling an ambulance.

Yeah, that sounds like the kind of thing she'd say.

– I'm Shirley, by the way, says Shirley. Shirley Gedanken.

– Wound Man.

– What?

– Wound Man. My name's Wound Man.

Shirley stops himself from saying that's a funny sort of name because what sort of a name for a boy is Shirley. But Wound Man sees the thought move behind Shirley's eyes.

– It's not my, what do you call it, my birth name. It's my… professional name.

– Right, says Shirley. What do you do, exactly?

– Oh, I'm… Freelance, says Wound Man. Portfolio career. Social intervention neck of the woods. Consultancy. Community.

Shirley's looking blank.

– Look, in layman's terms… I'm a sort of a… superhero. Could you pass me that pen?

– A superhero? says Shirley.

– And the sponsorship form, says Wound Man. – I'm afraid it'll take me a couple of minutes to do my signature, I'm right-handed and worst luck I have a rather floppity wrist.

– Like Superman? says Shirley. Not the wrist, I mean, the… superhero thing. Like a proper superhero. Like, what sort of, do you have, superpowers?

– Well, I don't fly, if that's what you mean. I'm not quite as aerodynamic as I'd like to be. One's practice is not so spectacular, anyway. It's rather more… grass roots. The sector's changed a lot in the last twenty years. We're more about sustainable engagement now. We're not just in and out. We try to apply a more dimensionalized perspective to the challenges we're dealing with. It's all about empowering other people really.

– Can you see through people's clothes though? says Shirley.

– No, says Wound Man. That's a rather more 70s vibe.

– Not even, like, women's bras and stuff?

– No, says Wound Man. Not… not… No. …Look I'm trying to write my name, belt up a sec. Your mother's right, you won't last two minutes with your cakehole shut.

– But do you… – Sorry, says Shirley. He tries to count to ten in his head.

One.

Two.

– But do you need a sidekick? Possibly? You've probably got one already. I just thought with the move and everything…

Wound Man looks up from the sponsorship form. He looks straight at Shirley with a kind of intensity that Shirley could easily believe was a superpower anyway. For a second or two Shirley feels more naked than if Wound Man could see through his clothes to his skin and through his skin to the goo on the inside.

Wound Man blinks once, twice. It makes no sound.

Shirley realizes with a jolt that there are tears in Wound Man's eyes. He looks away.

– Lovely kitchen, he says.

He looks at the postcard of the boy on the fridge door. In the picture, the boy is looking up and to his left, as if he's reading the proliferation of magnetic poetry that's stuck all over the fridge.

From where he's standing, Shirley can just about make out what the poetry says.

It says:

> **FUCK OUCH OW OH FUCK THIS HURTS**
> **OH OW OH SHIT THIS REALLY FUCKING HURTS**
> **IT HURTS IT HURTS OH SHIT WILL THIS NEVER**
> **END OW OW OW OW FUCK FUCK SHIT OUCH**

– So what do you think? says Wound Man.

– Sorry, what? says Shirley.

– This sponsored silence, says Wound Man. I don't know how much to put myself down for.

How long do you think you can go without talking?

Think about it, Shirley. It's going to be pretty … excruciating.

Think of all the things you might be dying to say.

Think of all the things that might be going on inside of you and all you want to do is speak about them.

How long do you think you can go before you have to say something?

A month? Two months?

Three.

Shirley's never been in so much pain. His legs, his chest, his heart in his chest, his lungs, he feels like he might just puke his own lungs up there on the grass. His head is pounding a quarter-second out of sync with his heart.

It's his heart hurts the worst.

But maybe it might all still be worth it…?

Except who's this bearing down on him?

It's Mr Carpenter-Finch in his yellow tracksuit.

He looks like a hairy convict trying to escape from a banana.

– Hold on a minute, Shirley, says Mr Carpenter-Finch, emergingly.

– Fuck off fuck off fuck off says Shirley I'll talk to you in a minute.

In his head, he says that.

– Hello Mr Carpenter-Finch, says Shirley. Is that a new tracksuit?

Mr Carpenter-Finch produces a smile from somewhere. All the kids ask him that, every week. He knows he's a joke. But they don't know him. They don't know the first thing about him.

– That was quite some run today, Shirley, says Mr Carpenter-Finch. I've never seen you pull out the stops like that. I thought you hated cross-country. You normally walk the last half.

– I just wanted to push myself, says Shirley.

– Good for you, lad, says Mr Carpenter-Finch.

Nobody ever calls Shirley 'lad'.

– You keep this up, we might have to think about trying you out for the team.

Shirley could cry, he feels it welling up inside him, he wonders what would happen if he cried, right now, if he just let go and cried.

It occurs to him that there's more than an outside chance that Mr Carpenter-Finch would cry too. And then they'd be crying together, and the only thing worse than that in the small part of Shirley's imagination that's reserved for scenarios concerning Mr Carpenter-Finch is if they somehow wound up in a sauna together.

Everything's totally ruined. Shirley knows it. He's sure of it.

It comes on to rain, just a spot.

Mr Carpenter-Finch starts to climb a bit back down into his banana, and zips it up as far as it will go.

– Well don't let me keep you, Shirley, says Mr Carpenter-Finch. Go and get a shower.

– Yes, sir, say the remains of Shirley. He knows deep down he's too late.

And sure enough, as he walks to the changing rooms, heart still pulsing in his neck like a lunatic flipping out and banging his head on the walls of a padded cell, Shirley looks up to see half a dozen boys in uniform coming the other way, bags slung easily over their shoulders, swearing at each other, doing their horseplay, and there in the middle of it all is…

The one.

He doesn't even see Shirley, which Shirley's glad about.

It's only fair. Cos Shirley didn't get to see him.

Shirley, who's run the cross-country race of his life with the single aim of making it back to the changing rooms in time to see...

The leaders, the pace-setters. The winners.

To see him. The one.

Stepping out of the shower.

Letting his body be utterly publicly visibly naked while he towels his hair dry.

Or at least in time to see him sitting around in his plain white underwear teasing his friends and putting on deodorant.

Or at least in time to see him putting his white school shirt back on that makes his skin look darker and the colour of his eyes more green.

Or at least in time to see the last-gasp glimpse of his nudity, as he sits on the bench and puts his socks on.

But no. It's too late.

He's gone.

Shirley's run his heart out and it's still not good enough.

He doesn't belong in a room with that much loveliness.

Shirley stands bent over with his hands on his knees, and wonders if he'll ever get his breath back. Or whether this time it's gone for good.

Four.

– Aren't you going to finish that? says Wound Man, pointing at Shirley's plate with a knife that he didn't come in with.

Two more fire engines go past outside the window.

Wound Man and Shirley are sitting either side of a table for two at a fast-food restaurant in town called OK Potato. It's like a vaguely trendy version of Spud-U-Like, but themed around Radiohead. Nobody who eats at OK Potato really wants to be eating there. Nobody's going to finish their potato.

– I think I've had enough, says Shirley. I wasn't very hungry in the first place.

Shirley's regretting having ordered the Blow Out.

Wound Man got the Fitter Happier. It's basically just a jacket potato with no butter and a load of cottage cheese. He may be fitter as a consequence but he doesn't seem to be looking any happier.

Shirley didn't think his first night on the job as trainee sidekick would start like this.

He slush-pumps the last of his Coke and they pay and go out. The balmy late spring evening air is rich with the sound of sirens. Fire, ambulance, it's all kicking off.

– They're playing our song, says Wound Man.

The two of them walk down the weirdly empty street in roughly the direction of the sound of the melee of emergency vehicles. Clankity-clunk, goes Wound Man, all tooled up to the nines.

– So what should I do when we get there, asks Shirley? He's a little nervous. He thinks he maybe should have mentioned earlier that he's not that great with heights. Or fighting.

– All you have to do for now, says Wound Man, is stand by my side, and watch what happens. Are you ready? We're nearly there.

Shirley feels a lurch in his stomach, which is mostly potato but a little bit nerves.

He realizes he can taste smoke.

They turn a corner.

– Oh Wound Man, says Shirley. We're too late.

There before them is an awful scene. There's been a big fire in a block of flats. The top half of the building is basically gutted, it's black and sparkling with the water from the fire hoses. Odd bits of the building are exposed, strange juts of structural teeth and crinoline. There must be a hundred and fifty people down here at street level, some of them still staring up at the fire that's over, as if in their heads it's still ablaze. Radios are chattering with jargon. Women and men are crying. Kids are crying too, or playing in the street, according to how much they're taking in.

One little girl, who's been splashing in the puddles with a pale blue plushy elephant jiggling in her grasp, catches sight of Wound Man and stops as dead as the world musical statues champion.

– No we're not, says Wound Man. We're not late at all. We're right on time. You watch.

And he slowly raises his right arm and waves his floppity hand at the girl.

She doesn't know whether to shriek or smile.

Neither does Shirley.

But slowly, gradually, the people gathered round start to turn their attention to Wound Man. There are gasps and whimpers and curse words – not propelled towards Wound Man, just tumbling out of their mouths.

A hush starts to descend.

– Is it a bird-scarer? says someone.

– Is it a plane wreck? says somebody else.

– No, says Wound Man. It's only me. It's Wound Man.

A boy, maybe ten years old, comes over. He looks up at Wound Man suspiciously.

– Are you real or what? says the kid.

He's become transfixed by the hole in Wound Man's side where the biggest of the swords goes in. Shirley's tried not to stare at that hole himself. It's the colour of smoky bacon. When you look at it you can taste the flavour of crisps.

– Can I put my finger in there? says the kid.

– If you want to, says Wound Man.

The boy grins nervously. He does something that neither Wound Man nor Shirley expects him to do. He licks his finger. And then he pokes it curiously, and not without a certain tenderness, into the wound in Wound Man's side.

A wonderful confusion blossoms in the young kid's face.

– My finger feels electric, he says.

– I know, says Wound Man.

– It's better, says the kid, than the time I stuck it in the dog. That was boring.

– I'm so pleased, says Wound Man.

All this has been happening very quietly, but still, everybody in the street is mesmerised. They've turned their backs on what's left of the block of flats. Only the occasional mutter of a walkie-talkie decorates the quiet.

– Thomas, says a woman. Come away from there now.

She's talking to the boy.

He goes, Awwww.

He's reluctant to step away from Wound Man. So the woman comes over. But as she approaches, the tension in her face just leaks away. By the time she's standing next to them, she's five years younger.

– I'm sorry about Thomas, she says.

– Don't worry, says Wound Man. It's perfectly all right.

– They're all a bit over-excited, with the fire, she says. It's all a big game when you're that age, isn't it. They don't understand. They don't know what's gone. They don't know what's ruined.

What are we going to do, she says.

– I'm afraid I don't know, says Wound Man. I'm so sorry.

Shirley looks at Wound Man's face, at the look in his eyes. The sadness there, the limitless melancholy. The blinkless stare of someone who's just had a very large portion of cottage cheese.

– No, I'm glad you're here, says the woman.

She's crying a bit but she smiles as she looks at him.

– To be honest, she says, you look how I feel.

Wound Man turns to Shirley, and whispers to him.

– That's it, he says. That's the superpower.

And then he turns back to the woman, and smiles.

– Can I introduce you to someone? This is my sidekick, says Wound Man. This is Shirley.

Five.

(Loud music. SHIRLEY bouncing around his bedroom playing air-guitar.)

Friday night, and Shirley's staying home, just making sure that the stars on his bedroom ceiling don't suddenly start glowing.

– SHIRLEY!

That's his dad from downstairs.

– TURN IT DOWN TO DEAFENING!

Shirley'd turn it up if he could, but it won't go any higher.

You know what's deafening, Shirley shouts at his dad. In his head.

The silence.

The silence of the secrets that get kept round here.

The silence of no music, no trumpet practice, coming from Tony's bedroom.

Which for some reason you and mum have started calling the spare room.

You horrible fucking bastards.

Shirley turns the music down.

His parents probably think he hates them cos they called him Shirley. He honestly couldn't care less any more. That was back when he was ten and Tony was fourteen and teasing him about it. These days he doesn't give a damn.

Apart from anything else…

It's the only thing they have in common.

Him and…

…the one, the boy he's completely hopelessly in love with, the prince of cross-country running.

He's the only other one at school with a funny name.

Do you know what it is? If you don't, you just have to know where to look.

Like, almost any page of Shirley's sketchbook, there you'll see it. Written a dozen times, a dozen fonts, a dozen ways.

His name is Subway.

Mr and Mrs Darling's only son, Subway.

Shirley Gedanken hearts Subway Darling. Two hundred thousand per cent.

Merry Christmas with all our love. From Shirley and Subway. Subway and Shirley. And the cats. Kiss.

Subway of course is a much cooler name than Shirley, and the kids at school don't know and Subway certainly isn't going to tell them that he's named after a song by Petula Clark.

Shirley only knows about the song because Wound Man told him.

A few days ago, this was. Shirley keeps replaying this conversation in his head.

– Petula Clark, says Wound Man. That takes me back.

They're sitting in a cafe called TNT, waiting for the rain to stop. Wound Man and Shirley have just been down on the high street, where a little girl was hit by a car. They were much too late to push her out of the way of the speeding vehicle but when, after a scary few minutes, she came round and the paramedics asked her where it hurt, she pointed at Wound Man and said: Over there.

– Petula Clark, says Wound Man again, as if her very name were Germolene.

He starts to sing; or not really.

– 'The lights are much brighter there, you can forget all your hmm-hmm, forget all your hair…'. I can't remember how it goes. That's not the same song, of course.

Wound Man smiles at Shirley and realizes that Shirley is shaking.

– I'm all right, says Shirley.

– Are not, says Wound Man.

– It's just that I've never told anyone before. About Subway. About… any of it.

– Well, thank you for telling me, says Wound Man.

– You don't mind? asks Shirley, wincing a bit. He almost wishes that Wound Man would mind.

– Why should I mind? says Wound Man.

– I thought you might not want a gay sidekick.

– Well, for one thing, says Wound Man, I have rather a large gay fan base. They go fruitloops for the St Sebastian look. And for another thing…

Wound Man stops. They listen to the sound of the rain outside for so long that Shirley begins to wonder if the rain is actually the other thing.

– What's the other thing? says Shirley, eventually.

– Well, look, don't take this the wrong way, says Wound Man. I don't mean anything by this. But… you're my fifth sidekick in the last two years. The rest were all teenage boys as well. There's a certain… Pattern.

Shirley takes a sip of his Coke. Wound Man's fiddling with the arrowhead that's stuck in his thigh.

– I don't understand, says Shirley. I don't know what you're trying to say.

– Let's drop it, says Wound Man.

The rain looks like it's never going to end. They might be stuck in this cafe forever.

– Shirley, says Wound Man.

– Wound Man, says Shirley.

– Tell me about my next-door neighbour, would you? Talk to me about Mr Parsley.

Six.

– Hey Tone, says Shirley.

He's sitting on his bed with the black moulded plastic case all cold on his bony knees.

– Tony, listen. I'm leading a secret double life. It's amazing. I can't tell anyone.

It's true. Nobody even suspects that Shirley's living such a complicated dual existence.

He's been pretty good about not opening the case but this morning the anxiety is just too unbearable. What if there's nothing left inside at all? He just needs to check that it hasn't completely disappeared.

He undoes the clips. Opens the lid and checks.

It takes two seconds.

Something at the back of Shirley's throat makes the smallest saddest sound.

He closes the lid.

It's still there. It's dwindling but it's there. For the moment.

He puts the case back underneath the bed.

Grabs a towel, and hits the shower.

These days, when the water hits his body, his body says, OK then. Let's do it.

Shirley's fallen into the strangest routine.

The stars, the case, the shower. No breakfast. The bus to school. He hangs out. Is officially the weirdest kid in his year. That's fine. He walks from class to class. Sometimes he's a genius, as if there are waves in his brain made of pure cosmic intelligence. Sometimes he's so out of it it's like he's in his own private stoner movie. Or one of those films where a mad inventor barricades himself in his garden shed and no one knows what he's building.

And then one afternoon a week he does cross-country running, and every week he comes in thirty seconds closer to Subway, and now he knows what Subway looks like when he's tying his shoelaces.

And then his homework's done on the bus, in a flurry of genius or a clot of bewildering nonsense. He wolfs his tea down before he even knows what he's eating. And then he announces he's going out. His parents call after him in a blur of reverb. He hasn't heard anything that either of them has said in days and days.

Wound Man and Shirley meet in the TNT, as a precaution against the surveillance of the Neighbourhood Watch. Reg Parsley's blinds have been twitching like it's 1999.

Shirley has a Coke and Wound Man has a cappuccino with a straw. And then they go out into the world and show up in the aftermath of every suburban atrocity in a twenty-mile radius. They've done toddlers down wishing wells and piglets up trees. Relationship break-ups and threshing accidents. Heart attacks, heads stuck in railings, and freak electrocutions at the local ice-rink. Everyone, everyone, is glad to see Wound Man. And Shirley couldn't be more proud.

Last thing at night, falling into bed and looking up at the stars, before he switches his light out, Shirley's head is awhirl with the night's adventures and the bone-white buttons on Subway's shirt and the names of their cats which will be Parachute and Funicular, and the ghost of the echo of the sound of Tony's trumpet practice from the other room.

It doesn't sound much like a routine, does it? But it is.

Until one day in the corridor, who should accost him but Mr Carpenter-Finch, in his tight brown catalogue suit.

– Have you got a moment, Shirley? says Mr Carpenter-Finch.

Shirley can't remember where he was going anyway.

– I expect you've heard about Paul Dickory. The captain of the Under-15s cross-country team. Done himself a mischief. Some peculiar incident at the ice rink.

– I wasn't there, says Shirley in a flash.

– No, no, says Mr Carpenter-Finch. The thing is, we've got an important inter-school meet at the weekend, we need to show up with a full complement of sixteen, and right now, we're not quite there. And given the improvement you've made, and more importantly the enthusiasm you've started to show for the sport, you were my obvious choice.

– For captain? says Shirley, who's struggling a bit to keep up.

– Hardly, says Mr Carpenter-Finch. No, Subway Darling will be captain. You'll be… making up the numbers. I mean, having an experience.

– No thanks, says Shirley.

– Good, says Mr Carpenter-Finch. I knew I could count on you, Shirley. The minibus leaves 8.30 Saturday morning.

And with that, Mr Carpenter-Finch is out through the double-doors and gone like a cowboy who just came out on top in a barroom brawl.

– I think you should do it, says Wound Man.

– Why? says Shirley.

– Well you said yourself that Subway doesn't ever speak to you. If you're on his running team, he'll have to pay attention to you, won't he?

– Actually, he's spoken to me now, says Shirley. A few days ago in chemistry I was staring at the back of his neck where his hair's all short and he turned round and saw me.

– And what did he say?

– He said, Fuck off you bender.

– There, well that's splendid, says Wound Man. He knows you're a bender already, that's an awkward conversation that you don't have to have.

Shirley smiles, though he feels a bit sad, and he chugs his Coke while Wound Man tries to get the last of his cappuccino to go round the neck of his bendy straw.

When Shirley eventually writes the next scene, which he will do, one day, but not until he's older, he'll start by putting this title at the top of the page:

The last time I ever saw my brother.

And then he'll cross it out because you shouldn't know that at the start.

Cos Shirley didn't know. What did Shirley know?

Hospital. People go in and out of hospital. It's nothing, just a thing.

When his mum and dad said, Why don't you spend some time with Tony, just you two boys, he thought fine, yeah, Tony's probably bored of watching telly.

It seemed like every time they went to see him, the TV was on, but never quite loud enough to hear. Just a little bit of colour and movement to show that time hadn't actually stopped.

This particular evening, Tony seemed tired, but he wanted Shirley to stay. Shirley didn't mind. There was nothing much else to do anyway.

Tony was propped up on pillows and Shirley had the chair by the bed. They were watching the synchronized swimming from who-knows-where.

The blue of the water, the whites of the smiles. None of it looked real.

Tony asked about school. There wasn't much to tell.

He asked about home. Ditto.

He asked about girls. It was a subject they'd never spoken about. Shirley was vague, so vague he felt hot and had to take his sweater off. Tony talked about this girl that Shirley had never heard of. To this day, Shirley doesn't know if this girl was at school or a movie star or someone down the chippy or totally imagined or what. She was just this girl, or really the idea of a girl, coming out of Tony in a long unravelling murmur.

Shirley never caught her name.

The blue of the water, the whites of the smiles.

Tony didn't want a Rolo. Oh Tony, said Shirley. You *are* sick. I am, said Tony.

The sound of the rest of the hospital outside, quieter than silence somehow.

– Shirley, said Tony. Can you do us a favour?

– Yeah, said Shirley.

– Would you mind looking after my trumpet? said Tony.

– Why? said Shirley.

– I just want to know that it's safe, said Tony.

– OK, said Shirley. You sure you don't want my last Rolo?

– Give it to someone you love, said Tony.

When Shirley eventually writes this all down, he'll stop at this point, for a breather. He'll want to describe how this feels, but he won't have the words. He'll be looking for an image. But he won't find the image for days.

And then, nodding off on the bus one evening, he'll suddenly remember a dream he had not long after Tony's funeral. The strangest dream of the world's most intelligent super-computer, singing to itself in an empty office in the middle of the night, so it won't be lonely.

(Music – a computer voice singing a sad song.)

Seven.

Mr Carpenter-Finch comes up to Shirley, Friday lunchtime.

– Get lots of sleep tonight, lad. You'll want to be fresh for tomorrow.

Shirley goes right off his sausage.

– Six o'clock Saturday morning and Wound Man and Shirley are slowly wearily clankity-clunking home. It's been a long night.

Do you want to come in? says Shirley. My parents are away, it's their anniversary. There's no one around. You can make sure I don't fall asleep. I've got be at school for half eight for this stupid running thing. Go on. Come in.

Shirley and Wound Man step inside.

Eight doors down, Reg Parsley reaches for his notebook and red felt pen. He writes with his tongue poking out. But he doesn't know that, and no one's ever told him. Actually, no one's ever noticed.

– This is my room, says Shirley, suddenly feeling a little bit shy.

– Very nice indeed, says Wound Man, looking around at the books and the pictures everywhere. Maps and photographs and clippings and cartoons and sketches that Shirley's obviously done himself. The whole room feels like one big three-dimensional diagram, like a blueprint. Somebody inventing a way to live.

– Stars on my ceiling. Stupid, says Shirley. Childish.

– Not a bit, says Wound Man. The wisest of men have always looked to the heavens for knowledge and inspiration.

Secretly, Wound Man agrees it's a little bit childish. In a sweet way. No harm. No harm except suddenly he's seeing how recently Shirley was younger than he is now, and how soon he's going to be older, he's sensing the slenderness of this exact moment in Shirley's life. The kind of slenderness that, when you see it in an actual body, your hand wants to go to it before you even know that it's true.

Shirley's packing his sportsbag.

– Shit, where are my socks, says Shirley.

Suddenly Wound Man understands more deeply than he ever has before how brave Shirley is. How brave they all are. His sidekicks.

Wound Man looks around the room, not especially for socks.

– What's this on your bed? says Wound Man.

Shirley's not even noticed it's there. He must have left it out when he went to school that morning.

– It's a trumpet case, says Shirley.

– I didn't know you played, says Wound Man.

– I don't, says Shirley, it belonged to my brother. He died last year. I'm supposed to take care of it.

Then he says something that Wound Man can't quite hear.

– What's that?

– I said I'm doing a rubbish job.

– How so?

Just for a moment, Shirley's throat twists in on itself and all he can do is pull a face.

He sits on the bed and puts the case on his knees. He can hardly stand the thought of even Wound Man being there to see this.

– Every time I open up the case…, says Shirley, I look at the trumpet, and it seems like it's got slightly smaller than the last time I looked. Like it's shrunk just a tiny bit. It does, it sounds mental. I'm sure I'm just imagining it.

He turns the case around to face Wound Man. He feels for the clips, opens them. Opens the lid. He can't even stand to look. He watches Wound Man's expression, not knowing what he hopes to see there.

Wound Man's expression doesn't change. But he tilts his head to one side a little, and then looks at Shirley.

– May I?

Shirley nods.

Wound Man reaches with his good arm down to the case, and carefully takes out the instrument.

It's a trumpet. Perfectly formed. But small. The size that a child's hand feels in yours when you cross the road together.

– That's not trumpet-size, is it, says Shirley.

– Probably not quite, no, says Wound Man. But the measure of a trumpet is the sound it makes. How does it sound?

– Don't know, says Shirley. I've never played it.

– Well that won't do, says Wound Man. C'mon, let's wake up the neighbourhood.

He puts the trumpet to his lips and starts to blow.

It makes no sound. Not a peep.

– Oh it doesn't even play, says Shirley. I've totally ruined it.

– No you haven't, says Wound Man. Listen. Carefully.

He blows down the mouthpiece again.

Shirley's aware of the slightest sensation like something's chopping up the air around his ears. It's silent but it's something.

– Shirley, says Wound Man.

– Wound Man, says Shirley.

– Be a love and open the window.

Shirley does as he's told, but he doesn't get it.

A third time Wound Man puts his lips to the trumpet and blows, and for a second or two there's just early Saturday morning.

Then the floor starts to shake below Shirley's feet.

It's an earthquake. Is it? It can't be.

It feels like a… sounds like a…

(The sound of a distant stampede of animals, getting gradually closer.)

Shirley swallows hard. He goes to the window. Now he gets it.

It's a stampede. The sound of animals for miles around, roused by this supersonic clarion call.

To begin with there's nothing to see except curtains twitching the length of the cul-de-sac.

Then Shirley sticks his head out of the window, as far as he can, and looks down the road. There at the end…

– Dogs, says Shirley.

Dozens and dozens of dogs.

Big ones, little ones, every species of dog, all tearing down the road like they're chasing the sexiest rabbit of their canine dreams.

– Oh wow, says Shirley. We've really done it now.

– Do you think I should stop? says Wound Man.

– No! says Shirley. Keep playing! It's awesome!

Wound Man puckers up again and blows some more.

– I've never seen anything like it, says Shirley. There must be like fifty dogs.

And it's not just dogs, there are cats mixed up in it too, all coming up the road like a fuzzy tornado. And –

– What the hell is that, says Shirley? Don't stop playing, it's…

(Music.)

Oh my God, it's an aardvark, Wound Man. You've summoned an aardvark. Coming down the road!

An aardvark followed by an alligator. Followed by a shedload of ants formed into the shape of an arrowhead.

Two debonair baboons. A company of badgers, Wound Man. A colony of bats overhead.

There's a juggling bear, and there's bees and birds and there's butterflies, Wound Man, endless butterflies.

An enigmatic camel, and fifteen chickens in a getaway car, and half a dozen chimpanzees dressed up like Reservoir Dogs.

A cockroach with a cow on a leash and a cartoon deer and a dolphin on stilts and a donkey eating an old straw hat.

Two little ducks doing rhythmic gymnastics and an eagle, oh God, Wound Man, look at that eagle up there!

There's an elephant doing a wheelie on a pushbike and an elk being chased by an emu. There's a bunch of ferrets in a human pyramid, I mean a ferret pyramid. There's finches and fishes and a big inflatable flamingo. There's a fox in bondage gear and a clutch of agoraphobic frogs looking dubious.

Look! There's a teeny tiny giraffe hitching a lift on a goose. There's a fat gorilla holding up a speech balloon that says 'This all seems a bit far-fetched to me'. There's a horde of hamsters making a break for it in their exercise wheels. Four hungry hungry hippos and a disco horse with a big gold medallion.

Hummingbirds, hummingbirds, Wound Man! And a hyena doing backflips and a jackal in spats. A jellyfish poking its head out of a kangaroo's pouch. And loads of deaf ladybirds who just got caught up in the excitement. A lamb and a lion who look like they're dating, and a llama on a spacehopper, going like the clappers.

There are monkeys with a banner that says END WAR NOW and an impetuous moose in pyjamas and some mice with a carving knife – that's a nice looking knife, eh, Wound Man.

Oh, God, Wound Man!

Are you all right?

Keep playing!

Something tells me we might be only half way through!

(Music swells.)

Eight.

Shirley in nothing but his boxers sits with his elbows on his knees and his chin in his hands. He's so bony.

From across the changing room, Subway Darling looks for the first time properly ever at Shirley Gedanken, the weirdest kid in the year.

– You nervous? says Subway.

I mean literally, seriously, those two words, in that order, come out of Subway Darling and fin their way through the grey changing room air and arrive at the ear of Shirley, who instantly forgets how to speak and what his name is and everything.

– You'll be all right, says Subway. All you have to do is put one foot in front of the other. Over and over and over again. For as long as it takes. You can do that, can't you?

Shirley finds he knows the answer to that one.

– Yeah, he says. I can do that.

For as long as it takes.

Yeah yeah.

– You'd better come in if you're coming, says Wound Man, and takes the old lady chain off the door.

– I'm sorry to intrude, says Reg. No doubt you're a busy man.

The kitchen feels smaller than ever.

— I'd offer you some tea, says Wound Man, but it hurts my wrist when I pick up the kettle.

— What *is* that? says Reg, pointing at Wound Man's floppity wrist. Bad case of RSI?

— Not quite, says Wound Man. But work-related, yes.

— Yes I've been wondering, says Reg. What is your work, exactly?

— Consultancy, says Wound Man. Freelance.

— And that requires those snazzy pants, does it?

— No, says Wound Man. It requires pants. I require the snazz.

— And what about your little friend?

Here we go, thinks Wound Man.

— I don't know what you mean.

— Yeah you do, says Reg. The Gedanken boy. The older one died not that long since, you know. That's a very vulnerable family. I don't know quite what your interest in the young one is.

— Professional, says Wound Man. Purely professional.

The reason that Wound Man hates the Reg Parsleys of the world is that he has to lie to them. Because they can't hear anything complicated. They don't understand that it's not all black and white. So he has to talk white. And they all hear black regardless.

Reg surveys the kitchen. The postcard of the boy on the fridge.

— That another one, is it?

— Another one what? says Wound Man.

— I'm sure I shouldn't like to say, says Reg.

Every weapon in Wound Man's body feels like it just went in.

— I take it you've never had a sidekick, Mr Parsley, says Wound Man. You don't have the air of a man who's ever had a sidekick.

Reg just smiles. Wound Man's seen that smile so many times and every time he understands it a little bit less.

— Well I won't hold you up any longer, says Reg. Now that we've had this little conversation, I'm sure you'll have a lot that you need to get done in a short space of time.

— Indeed, says Wound Man. Well there we are. A superhero's work is never done.

No one's overtaken Shirley for ages. Which either means that he's holding his position, or he's last.

Everything inside him right now is the same thing. For once he's coherent, he's one thing, he's all about the one thing.

One foot in front of the other. Over and over and over again.

He's never understood that expression before: to give something your all.

All of him is given over to this.

For as long as it takes.

There are signals of pain that he has to not recognize yet. Maybe later. For now they just have to be sorted into a rhythm. And then he has to lock himself into the rhythm.

He's never felt what it's like to give everything.

This is what it's like.

To hold nothing in reserve.

He's giving the whole of his body to the captain of his team, he's yielding it up.

The rhythm of the pain for as long as it takes.

He's giving the whole of his body to Subway Darling.

Shirley Gedanken's just a ghost left behind in the background.

Maybe this is what it feels like to be Tony.

It's dark by the time the team leave the pizza place. Mr Carpenter-Finch on the strength of one glass of wine has lost it completely and burst into tears while attempting, in the midst of an impromptu speech, to say the word 'creditable'. 'A creditable third place overall'.

Mr Bluefold and Mr Carpenter-Finch quietly decide that maybe Mr Bluefold should drive Mr Carpenter-Finch's car on the way back.

Then Shirley overhears Mr Bluefold suggest to Subway that maybe, as captain, he'd like to travel with them in the car instead of on the minibus.

So Shirley, summoning the courage from somewhere –
somewhere apparently new – asks Mr Bluefold if he can go
in the car with them too.

– I get sick in the minibus, says Shirley. I'm sure I'd be fine
in the car.

(Music underneath.)

And so as Mr Bluefold puts his foot down, with the
motorway lights going past above their heads like a Morse
code message from the universe, there in the back seat
together at last sit the opposite poles of the Under-15 cross-
country team. Shirley and Subway, Subway and Shirley.
Cats not pictured. And no kiss. At least for the moment.

Neither of them says a word to the other. Subway's asleep
within minutes.

At first, Shirley can't even look at him. He stares out of
the window, watching the middle of nowhere scroll past
his eyes, and the occasional electric word attached to a
superstore.

And then, slowly, softly, Shirley lets his eyes turn to
Subway, sleeping. The light on his face, then the darkness,
then the light. The nothing in his face but being there. The
blatant nearness of his skin to the rest of the world. The
total undefended honesty of Subway asleep.

Shirley's going to watch Subway sleeping all the way home,
even for a second or two after Subway wakes up and
notices Shirley watching.

That will all happen, but this little bit of the story ends
about fifty miles back up the motorway, when Shirley,
watching Subway sleeping, says to himself: Wherever we're
going, we'll get there.

And it's bliss in his heart.

Mr Bluefold turns up the music on the car CD player.

(Music swells.)

And a hundred miles away, in Shirley's darkling bedroom, in the empty house, on the silent cul-de-sac, on Shirley's ceiling, with no one to see it, the stars are all glowing like a thousand fireflies.

Nine.

– I don't know why you're bellowing like a savage through the letterbox at ten p.m. in the evening, says Reg Parsley. Your pal's been called away. Family emergency.

Shirley's trying to remember where Wound Man said there was a spare front door key.

– He doesn't have any family, Mr Parsley, says Shirley.

He remembers about the hanging basket, and reaches up to find the key.

– Well he went off in a taxi a good hour and a half ago, says Reg.

– He wouldn't have, says Shirley, there's no way, and he lets himself into the house.

In the hall, the boxes of stuff that Wound Man was still unpacking are all present and correct.

– Wound Man? calls Shirley, into the dead air of the house.

In the kitchen, instinctively Shirley knows that there's something different, but it takes him a second or two to figure out what it is.

On the fridge door, no postcard of the dead boy actor. And almost all of the magnetic poetry gone.

In its place, a note, in spidery writing.

It says: Shirley, Time to move on. I'm sorry. All my love, always. WM.

Fixed to the fridge with the single magnetic word OUCH.

Out in the hall again, bristling with tears, Shirley realizes that the boxes that Wound Man was unpacking have all been resealed with tape.

This is not, mutters Shirley to himself, how any story's going to end that has him as a principal character.

Shirley counts out twenty, thirty, forty pounds into the taxi driver's palm. Keep the change, he says, feeling like a bigshot. The change is literally 50p.

He runs through the automatic doors into the terminal. Thousands of people all going where they're going. The sky, mostly. All going off into the sky.

Shirley looks up at the departure screens. Has he done the right thing by guessing on the airport? Where on earth would Wound Man be going? The sheer number of possible destinations in itself feels as big as a religion, the kind of religion that needs you to feel small.

He's just going to have to have a look.

And so, for the second time in one day, with his whole body arguing against it, Shirley is all about the running. Haphazard and graceless this time and stumbling and directionless and panicking and lost and all of the other words that have to do with love.

Up one escalator, down the next, following signs that have nothing to do with him. Arrivals, departures. He stops for a moment. Calm down, Shirley. What would Wound Man do?

He has no idea.

All these people, the signs and the diagrams, the vastness of the terminal, it's all too much, it's making him dizzy. He closes his eyes and tries to breathe.

Tannoy announcements in made-up languages. Muzak and pinball and kids kicking off. The hum of the escalators. Planes taking off outside. All of it just for a moment recedes and there in the midst of the mix is his answer.

Clankity-clunk, goes Wound Man.

That's all that Shirley needs to know.

He gets his breath back just in time.

WOUND MAN! says Shirley.

Shirley? says Wound Man. He's just spat cappuccino everywhere.

His eyes go straight to Shirley on the floor below, and the sign above Shirley's head that says 'meeting point'.

He leans on the railing and waves his floppity hand at Shirley. Shirley sees Wound Man and he squeaks inside like a toy.

Shirley bounds up the escalator to the cafe where Wound Man's been reading the paper and collecting his thoughts, and it's only at the very last minute that he stops himself throwing his arms around Wound Man. He can't, for obvious reasons, but the hugging energy surges uncontainably inside him and he ends up hugging himself.

(Background music from the cafe.)

– What's happened, Wound Man? says Shirley. What did you mean it's time to move on?

– Mr Parsley came to see me this morning, says Wound Man.

– Fuck Parsley, says Shirley. He doesn't know.

– No, he doesn't, says Wound Man. But I've been here before. A few times. To stay would be harmful. That's not what I want.

They talk a little about Shirley's day, about the race and the feeling and Subway asleep. They talk about some of the adventures they've had. They talk about the animals rampaging down the cul-de-sac. And then Wound Man says, Look, Shirley, I'd better go.

Wound Man stands up. Shirley stands too.

– Please, says Shirley. He can feel them inside him. All the things it's too excruciating not to say.

(The background music from the cafe building underneath.)

– Please, he says. Don't go. I don't know whether you understand what you've done. Because perhaps you can't see it. It's inside me. But it's made me different. I remember the morning I first saw you, out of my bedroom window. I'd just woken up and looked at the stars and that worked for a bit but then I thought the second thing and the third thing. The second thing was Tony and the third thing was Subway and day after day till the day I met you that's all there was. Just Tony and Subway. The two boys I loved till it hurt. It hurt because I couldn't touch them. I couldn't hold Tony and say goodbye. I couldn't put my hand on Subway's body. I couldn't actually touch them, Wound Man, neither of them. And then I became your sidekick and I saw you touching people without touching them. Does that make any sense? I saw you touch them and they touched you and yet no one touches you. How can I say this? You've never touched me but all the time I feel your arms around me and I feel you holding me, kissing me, I feel so safe in your arms, and it's never even happened, Wound Man, but it happens anyway. And I looked at

Subway sleeping and I realized this is how you look at me and I realized when I look at you I feel less scared and it's only because you look how I feel. And I know you've got to go but I really wish you didn't because you make me braver, Wound Man. You make me want to be brave.

(The cafe music recedes again.)

In his head, he says that. It's all inside him, and it's totally excruciating. But the words won't come.

– Please, he says. Send me a postcard.

– Of course, says Wound Man, who obviously knows everything that Shirley can't find the words for anyway. Because what's a superhero without telepathy? Just some div in a thong.

– I'll be right here, says Wound Man, and goes to touch Shirley on the forehead like E.T. touches Elliott. Only a spasm of pain shoots down his right arm and he twats Shirley in the face with the end of a spear.

– Oh, sorry, says Wound Man, oh God.

– Don't worry, says Shirley. It's fine.

– But that's going to be a black eye in the morning, says Wound Man.

– Yeah, says Shirley, and he grins.

They stand side-by-side on the down escalator, the two of them together for the last time, sharing a silence.

Shirley and Wound Man. Wound Man and Shirley.

– Look, I'd better go, says Wound Man. My flight's not for ages but it takes me for ever to get through security.

– Course, says Shirley.

– To be honest, says Wound Man, it's at times like these, I rather regret getting my cock pierced.

He picks up his bag.

– Look after yourself, says Wound Man. It's a huge responsibility for one so young.

– What is? says Shirley.

Wound Man smiles.

– Being the neighbourhood superhero, he says, and he turns and goes.

Clankity-clunk.

Shirley's skint, he's spunked all his money on the taxi down, it's going to take him all night to walk back home. But he's got all night.

The night is beautiful and clear and the sky is enormous and the stars are far away.

Shirley walks a bit, and runs a bit, and cries a bit, and walks and cries and walks and walks and runs a bit and stops and sits down and cries.

And he cries and cries and the sky is enormous and he wonders if every plane of the thousand planes he hears is Wound Man's plane and he gets up and walks a bit more. And he sings along to the trumpet tune in his head and he laughs and stops laughing and the city holds him right where he is, on the outskirts of his life, walking homewards, one foot in front of the other, over and over and over again, and he's got all night.

It's just about six o'clock as he turns into his cul-de-sac, humming his trumpet tune as dawn breaks around him and the birds go totally apeshit because everything's different now. Everything's changed.

He lets himself into the empty house and even though it's empty he creeps upstairs. He opens the door of his bedroom. The window's still open from the morning's stampede and the trumpet case is still on the bed. He puts it away with care, and closes the blind so his room's half-dark. He takes off his clothes and lies down on the bed looking up at the stars.

Everything's changed, thinks Shirley.

And in his mind he starts to rename all the constellations.

(Music building through to the end of the list.)

The Big Dagger and the Little Dagger. The Cutlass and the Battleaxe. Shrapnel and the Scimitar. The Shortsword and the Mace.

The Tiny Giraffe and the Bone-White Buttons.

The Synchronized Swimmers and the Debonair Baboons.

The Bird-Scarer and the Plane-Wreck.

The Incredible Shrinking Trumpet. Parachute and Funicular. Petula Clark and the Dead Boy Actor. The Electric Finger and the Dolphin on Stilts.

The Vegetable Knife and the Broken-Off Arrowhead.

The Javelin and the Morning Star.

(The music starts dwindling away.)

And as he renames the heavens, inevitably Shirley Gedanken drifts off to sleep, and falls headlong into a dream of flying – out through the open window, over the twitchy-curtained cul-de-sac, out over the city, crossing the flightpaths of the thousand aeroplanes, deep into space to the furthest edge of the universe, right up to the limits of what it's possible to dream.

What he doesn't know is, just the other side of those limits, that's where we all are, me and all of you, all watching him sleep. The light on his face, the dark, the light.

Wherever he's going, he'll get there.

(The briefest moment of absolute silence.)

Good night.

(Blackout. Music.)